Other Books

Sketches from the Hawaiian Archipelago, A Collection of Short Stories

Tellings of Aloha, Songs from Hawai‘i, A Collection of Poems

From Point A to C to Y to B:
A Sentimental Journey Through Hawai‘i and Wisconsin

155 Shakespearean Love Sonnets

* * * * *

The Closest Shave, A 3rd Lieutenant David Chan Mystery

One Halloween in Honolulu, A 2nd Lieutenant David Chan Mystery

Follie: The Disappearances of Honolulu, A Lieutenant David Chan Mystery

866 Love Haiku

by Lanning C. Lee

For all my Co-Workers ever

from Dole Cannery to the KOKUA Program

Text Copyright © 2017, 2022
by Lanning C Lee

Honolulu, Hawaiʻi
All Rights Reserved

Visit my author's site: LanningLee com
Amazon site: amazon com/author/LanningLee
Email me: LanningLee@gmail com

Table of Contents

1 green buds thrive in spring *1*
2 I give you my love *1*
3 in love's pure circumference *1*
4 for only true love *1*
5 never-changing love *2*
6 summer's mellow months *3*
7 when love's so perfect *3*
8 moving on in time *3*
9 days fly quickly past *3*
10 fall so short in love *4*
11 love knows its boundaries *5*
12 your hand clasping mine *5*
13 winter walks at night *5*
14 red on white canvass *5*
15 days fall into years *6*
16 love asks no favors *7*
17 in fond remembrance *7*
18 what is more than love *7*
19 hate is more than love *7*
20 hate is less than love *8*
21 never-changing love *9*
22 when love's so perfect *9*
23 moving on in time *9*
24 days fly quickly past *9*

25 orange on gray canvass 10
26 never-changing love 11
27 not find true love here 11
28 days fall into years 11
29 in warming to love 11
30 in silence love grows 12
31 enduring all blows 13
32 forget about love 13
33 a caress so soft 13
34 if it's true love's blind 13
35 love is blind to faults 14
36 you see love is blind 15
37 love thrives to the end 15
38 if love were so true 15
39 love is kind and true 15
40 when in love beware 16
41 love chooses those whom 17
42 love cannot decide 17
43 love may let us down 17
44 in the end with love 17
45 love will always look 18
46 hollow sounds echo 19
47 love is changeable 19
48 though we may forget 19
49 without love to heal 19
50 when true love is lost 20
51 love's warm daylight hours 21

52 *hate makes war on love* *21*
53 *then when love passes* *21*
54 *to love in the end* *21*
55 *then hate spawns new fears* *22*
56 *with nothing to lose* *23*
57 *for some this is truth* *23*
58 *love will stand steadfast* *23*
59 *love moves on in time* *23*
60 *love weakens in those* *24*
61 .... *25*
if love can feel pain *25*
62 *breathe hope while you sleep* *25*
63 *dangerous and wild* *25*
64 *love cannot be tamed* *25*
65 *love is perilous* *26*
66 *if only our love knew* *27*
67 *when love's game is won* *27*
68 *blinding our reason* *27*
69 *give over all you have* *27*
70 *if time healed all wounds* *28*
71 *distracting desire* *29*
72 *if it were easy* *29*
73 *lingering perfume* *29*
74 *even in our dreams* *29*
75 *lasting an instant* *30*
76 *never seen again* *31*
77 *maybe once in life* *31*

78	may be missed by chance	31
79	it can hardly be	31
80	lasting forever	32
81	strengthened through kind time	33
82	a journey for love	33
83	love that stands so strong	33
84	marking time with joy	33
85	fresh celebrations	34
86	each and every year	35
87	mellowing the time	35
88	once can be enough	35
89	who knew love's passing	35
90	and at the end we	36
91	no steel bars can stop	37
92	she embodies love	37
93	first holding my hand	37
94	she dazzles dark ways	37
95	her love is my sun	38
96	she has all my love	39
97	her love is like fire	39
98	should she leave me now	39
99	when she turns the game	39
100	she was once true love	40
101	even at the end	41
102	she lives beyond love	41
103	the brush of her hand	41
104	If I tried harder	41

105	when love looks for us	42
106	if love cradles us	43
107	love's security	43
108	love at any price	43
109	love is not for sale	43
110	if only love would	44
111	love's sure permanence	45
112	love's impermanence	45
113	love can last enough	45
114	love cannot last long	45
115	love makes no promise	46
116	words make hot desire	47
117	all love's fitful dreams	47
118	day's brilliant sunset	47
119	night's secrets warn love	47
120	of all of the kinds	48
121	if love conquers all	49
122	love's high barricades	49
123	love and violence	49
124	with love at first sight	49
125	two separate hearts	50
126	what do you call love	51
127	where is love hidden	51
128	of those loves gone by	51
129	when love looks away	51
130	romantics believe	52
131	a September thought	53

132	all you need is love	53
133	only preachers talk	53
134	Willie Nelson's song	53
135	love's true bluish light	54
136	Joni Mitchell sings	55
137	love is for the strong	55
138	of all things likely	55
139	Young also says love	55
140	it's only my love	56
141	in her careful hands	57
142	her intent to please	57
143	setting it apart	57
144	hides in a new breast	57
145	never to regain	58
146	still I seek it now	59
147	cannot always hide	59
148	away from me still	59
149	fly so far afield	59
150	rarely coming home	60
151	coming not to me	61
152	leaves no hope for me	61
153	with a love gone by	61
154	the heart knows true love	61
155	love meets resistance	62
156	love's clear and pure tone	63
157	the strong music of love	63
158	love knows no music	63

159 meet love halfway since 63
160 love makes plain intent 64
161 love gives no warning 65
162 we all know it's true 65
163 never holding back 65
164 love hurts and love kills 65
165 if love could happen 66
166 we once were lovers 67
167 love's a healing thing 67
168 love's a drastic thing 67
169 love's a noisy thing 67
170 love's a lively thing 68
171 love's a colored thing 69
172 love's a drastic thing 69
173 love's a brittle thing 69
174 love's a hearty thing 69
175 love's a hurtful thing 70
176 love's a manic thing 70
177 love's an active thing 70
178 love's a passive thing 70
179 love's a wondrous thing 71
180 love's a heady thing 71
181 love's a fruitful thing 72
182 love's a baffling thing 72
183 love's a wondrous thing 72
184 love's a hurting thing 72
185 loves a gentle thing 73

186	*with love's doubt I have*	*74*
187	*love's a caustic thing*	*74*
188	*love if to be found*	*74*
189	*love's a reckless thing*	*74*
190	*the slope so steepend*	*75*
191	*love's a careful thing*	*76*
192	*in search of love I*	*76*
193	*love's a brutal thing*	*76*
194	*love's sole fault to miss*	*76*
195	*love's a tender thing*	*77*
196	*love is blown to me*	*78*
197	*love's an artful thing*	*78*
198	*love's blasted going*	*78*
199	*love's a funny thing*	*78*
200	*the women you've known*	*79*
201	*love's a saddening thing*	*80*
202	*in love's high fever*	*80*
203	*love's a curious thing*	*80*
204	*in love's fine passion*	*80*
205	*love's a serious thing*	*81*
206	*rumors of demise*	*82*
207	*love's a wanting thing*	*82*
208	*when love is so kind*	*82*
209	*love's a tender thing*	*82*
210	*I've had many loves*	*83*
211	*love's a distant thing*	*84*
212	*of all that's in play*	*84*

213	*longing for your love*	84
214	*spring flowers bring renewal*	84
215	*vigorous of heart*	85
216	*the promise of my love*	86
217	*love's a comely thing*	86
218	*every love that's passed*	86
219	*not meant for your ears*	86
220	*for love gone wanting*	87
221	*boldly strutting by*	88
222	*love astonishes*	88
223	*love's a vivid thing*	88
224	*love's purest embrace*	88
225	*love's a dazzling thing*	89
226	*longing for a heart*	90
227	*love's a rapturous thing*	90
228	*love lasting for good*	90
229	*love's a stubborn thing*	90
230	*for you my dear love*	91
231	*if I did love you*	92
232	*that the past were now*	92
233	*at first sight of you*	92
234	*love reared my desire*	92
235	*to love you always*	93
236	*often in love's chance*	94
237	*my life without you*	94
238	*when love's on the run*	94
239	*a life without love*	94

240	in love forever	95
241	and when it's over	96
242	with love spinning round	96
243	love is a small gift	96
244	to help us find grace	96
245	painting a rainbow	97
246	all of love's colors	98
247	beyond mere beauty	98
248	of all we hold dear	98
249	love should never cease	98
250	wanting nothing more	99
251	love drives sleep away	100
252	with love comes marriage	100
253	wedding vows commit	100
254	in this life we seek	100
255	eternal love is	101
256	love's truth is nothing	102
257	to solve love's mystery	102
258	young love does not know	102
259	love is born where you	102
260	one truth about love	103
261	in no way does love	104
262	for some just one chance	104
263	some lovers might say	104
264	love tears at my heart	104
265	if love doesn't hurt	105
266	would that love would speak	106

267 in the days gone by 106

268 I thought of no end 106

269 I almost touched it 106

270 nearly in my grasp 107

271 love's dear memories 108

272 if only I could 108

273 a love beyond price 108

274 what will be with love 108

275 if it can be found 109

276 love light my way home 110

277 shining in the night 110

278 visions of the sun 110

279 love is wonderful 110

280 love is terrible 111

281 it is worth the pain 112

282 to love or love not 112

283 that fiery passion 112

284 burning with passion 112

285 minding my love's way 113

286 worried she may leave 114

287 my love is sweet rain 114

288 love's a thunderstorm 114

289 love's a freezing snow 114

290 my love's a warning 115

291 If my love offends 116

292 love in the present 116

293 love is imperfect 116

294 every love's different 116
295 a full quiver slays 117
296 to sustain my love 118
297 many fractured loves 118
298 love in the moment 118
299 after I gambled 118
300 to come to that point 119
301 I said I loved her 120
302 forgotten by love 120
303 proing and conning 120
304 in love's strangling thrall 120
305 love seeks to placate 121
306 love we have been so 122
307 when love is real we're 122
308 if love's on the wing 122
309 love is so reserved 122
310 we surely become 123
311 and as we grow up 124
312 once or twice I have 124
313 when I saw you last 124
314 often heartbroken 124
315 love has taken me 125
316 love's sometimes written 126
317 love could tell me now 126
318 love sees with bright eyes 126
319 forgotten at last 126
320 If love were once mine 127

321	a cursory glance	128
322	steeped in no love here	128
323	love finds me mindful	128
324	in a giving time	128
325	to storm on my love	129
326	with love unruly wild	130
327	love takes its chances	130
328	the ultimate love	130
329	placing our love held	130
330	I'm in this fine game	131
331	all love engenders	132
332	for us a caged love	132
333	A false love would fail	132
334	when love comes to us	132
335	with little chance of	133
336	if a heart finds me	134
337	if a new love comes	134
338	in finding new love	134
339	when my true love comes	134
340	love's game lies ahead	135
341	if love were so clear	136
342	perhaps you have found	136
343	to feel love's true fire	136
344	love stood still in time	136
345	hope for good fortune	137
346	in love's soft embrace	138
347	to run here and there	138

348 *to find love at last* *138*
349 *a path to pleasure* *138*
350 *dear love's secrets are* *139*
351 *love I'll tell you what* *140*
352 *then I had not seen* *140*
353 *light and lively we* *140*
354 *love taking all forlorn* *140*
355 *fair soul of an hour* *141*
356 *with night skies coming* *142*
357 *love sports in the sun* *142*
358 *when love's in full bloom* *142*
359 *no rude disturbance* *142*
360 *should love chance high seas* *143*
361 *a wedding vow sounds* *144*
362 *a brief affair would* *144*
363 *love's sweet voice is soft* *144*
364 *on a gentle breeze* *144*
365 *love's sidelong glance tells* *145*
366 *I've always heard that* *146*
367 *only favored ones* *146*
368 *when lover's hearts freeze* *146*
369 *one warm gentle word* *146*
370 *it's love's path to know* *147*
371 *love holds on not fast* *148*
372 *with love tearing deep* *148*
373 *in love's tough game play* *148*
374 *we would give the world* *148*

375	*in love's toughest times*	*149*
376	*though sometimes it ends*	*150*
377	*love stretched out at ease*	*150*
378	*love sends its soft dream*	*150*
379	*to grow its progress*	*150*
380	*in indifference*	*151*
381	*fully blinded I*	*152*
382	*love shot its arrow*	*152*
383	*I wandered awhile*	*152*
384	*then love did find me*	*152*
385	*all loves who've passed by*	*153*
386	*sick to lose love now*	*154*
387	*and the truest heart*	*154*
388	*love is to behold*	*154*
389	*love will surely come*	*154*
390	*love's a drop of light*	*155*
391	*the joy of love glows*	*156*
392	*solid permanence*	*156*
393	*why then confusion*	*156*
394	*love's coming rapture*	*156*
395	*love's oh so gentle*	*157*
396	*love can make you do*	*158*
397	*some heavy lightness*	*158*
398	*love does amaze in*	*158*
399	*dazzled eyes glowing*	*158*
400	*love's gone and what's left*	*159*
402	*in love's increasing*	*160*

403	in the course toward joy	160
404	in current dawning	160
405	that love is now mine	161
406	dreamless morning light	162
407	when the joys of love	162
408	in dear times now passed	162
409	now long forgotten	162
410	my sweet love rose up	163
411	in my dreams I dream	164
412	when my spirit's weak	164
413	when love has been there	164
414	loves blazing by me	164
415	with each passing love	165
416	radiant visions	166
417	for all you desire	166
418	she was kind to me	166
419	she says she loves me	166
420	for the hoped truth is	167
421	if the truth be told	168
422	if amid tumult	168
423	do we choose our love	168
424	love looks not with eyes	168
425	love's chaos in haste	169
426	the truth of it this	170
427	love's sublime being	170
428	with love's speaking now	170
429	with my heart pounding	170

430	and blissful is he	171
431	ascend highest heights	172
432	pale love sickly stood	172
433	just beyond my reach	172
434	she did not speak but	172
435	that night's perfect love	173
436	unreflecting love	174
437	of love it is said	174
438	in fast times of joy	174
439	pen and paper then	174
440	love I'm here waiting	175
441	love's warming embrace	176
442	when love breaks down doors	176
443	a holy message sent	176
444	love can open eyes	176
445	when new love takes wing	177
446	when love's flame burns bright	177
447	let love in dark skies	177
448	love soon puts to flight	177
449	with love's great power	178
450	whirling us away	178
451	how I recovered	179
452	memories of love	179
453	love in now old times	179
454	of long timeless love	179
455	lost along the way	180
456	bright stars flash so cold	181

457	so nearing true love	181
458	survey love's pathway	181
459	the red leaves rustling	181
460	a stammered word heard	182
461	try finding some love	183
462	stuttering desire	183
463	strong passion's embrace	183
464	blinded by desire	183
465	strangled in mid-air	184
466	take me to love's bounds	185
467	start the mad shouting	185
468	love's a blessed song	185
469	wandering down paths	185
470	my spirit rising	186
471	groping past the gloom	187
472	some distant discord	187
473	love whispered to me	187
474	love once said to me	187
475	love in the small hours	188
476	in long solitude	189
477	if it should pass me	189
478	now my love has passed	189
479	a steepening climb	189
480	nature's hardest test	190
481	love lifts me upward	191
482	love swiftly follows	191
483	if it were the case	191

484 the Ishiharas 191
485 innocent love comes 192
486 love's pictures play out 193
487 tentative in deed 193
488 imagined great love 193
489 in love's purest form 193
490 in love a bright match 194
491 with greatest promise 195
492 I've heard it said that 195
493 loving you always 195
494 love's fading embers 195
495 I've come to that point 196
496 now so sweet love has 197
497 that time when fairy 197
498 could only lost love 197
499 nothing of love would 197
500 love's longing victims 198
501 hoping for some love 199
502 love's first soft footsteps 199
503 hailing your advance 199
504 rare purified gold 199
505 a grand profusion 200
506 fading fast away 201
507 love's sensuousness 201
508 love's seductive stare 201
509 find a love that stays 201
510 truly wondrous love 202

511 in my memory 203
512 love so draws my eye 203
513 to find perfect love 203
514 gently love did come 203
515 hinting pains to come 204
516 a strange compression 205
517 if a love does fade 205
518 fiery yesterdays 205
519 with that chance meeting 205
520 her long dark black hair 206
521 the glories of love 207
522 long are we seekers 207
523 love's burning passion 207
524 in love we do bound 207
525 love may call to us 208
526 in love we may seek 209
527 high hopes of sweet love 209
528 a calling to believe 209
529 a plan that's fulfilled laid in sure simplicity 209
530 there may be times when 210
531 tried and so tired 211
532 dreaming I might love 211
533 seeking love this way 211
534 love's glance cools me now 211
535 all my grand conquests 212
536 love beckoned me once 213
537 singing love's strong bond 213

538	*just barely touching*	213
539	*starry nights so clear*	213
540	*burning hazily*	214
541	*we were pure and shone*	215
542	*I dreamt that love came*	215
543	*sometimes losing love*	215
544	*icing love crackled*	215
545	*crafted light and shade*	216
546	*love's worn and tired prints*	217
547	*lost love's fading glow*	217
548	*in love's swift high stream*	217
549	*searing our senses*	217
550	*so hard to believe*	218
551	*a romantic quest*	219
552	*in memory traced*	219
553	*a joyous delight*	219
554	*love's intentioned heart*	219
555	*promised fruition*	220
556	*that winged messenger*	221
557	*now a newfound love*	221
558	*when love comes near me*	221
559	*love long flown away*	221
560	*I lost my love then*	222
561	*when love will show me*	223
562	*unpracticed lovers*	223
563	*flown love stops my heart*	223
564	*those chaste devotions to find love's holiest times*	223

565	*those slow burning prayers*	*224*
566	*all should step forward*	*225*
567	*my love lost in time*	*225*
568	*mesmerized by you*	*225*
569	*love stirs skipped heartbeats*	*225*
570	*You will not know why*	*226*
571	*stunned backward by love*	*227*
572	*love's shy sidelong glance*	*227*
573	*smooth rhythms in time*	*227*
574	*running away fast*	*227*
575	*unfolding petals*	*228*
576	*sweetest love appears*	*229*
577	*love's variety*	*229*
578	*the faintest motion*	*229*
579	*love serves all delights*	*229*
580	*fantasy of light*	*230*
581	*round of love's potion*	*231*
582	*a toss of the dice*	*231*
583	*never-ending love*	*231*
584	*love lifted me up*	*231*
585	*led by sacred vows*	*232*
586	*searching for some love*	*233*
587	*lost relationships*	*233*
588	*when love is so strong*	*233*
589	*passionate spirit*	*233*
590	*now love's latter days*	*234*
591	*what makes love turn so*	*235*

592	*breaking hearts like glass*	235
593	*imagined heaven*	235
594	*on love's gentle might*	235
595	*some poets will boast*	236
596	*lost love's chilled hands grope*	237
597	*move out and away*	237
598	*an abandoned love*	237
599	*had I lived in awe*	237
600	*love's hot amber flame*	238
601	*in our sometime past*	239
602	*for all that's heart longed*	239
603	*floating forever*	239
604	*as I lay dreaming*	239
605	*now more than ever*	240
606	*in my distress now*	241
607	*of neglected love*	241
608	*oh dissembling love*	241
609	*how was I to know*	241
610	*You think you've found it*	242
611	*only love could know*	243
612	*in moments of loss*	243
613	*I looked on certain*	243
614	*at the bitter end*	243
615	*for now or never*	244
616	*so like common dust*	245
617	*a real love long lost*	245
618	*You won't know her love*	245

619	I was wrong about love	245
620	love's fondest embrace	246
621	love don't let me go	247
622	in a playful mood	247
623	a turn of shoulder	247
624	to give two pleasure	247
625	he awaits the spell	248
626	listening for a hint	249
627	a burning hot sleep	249
628	fan me with wide wings	249
629	this is too far off	249
630	love's crystal clear eyes	250
631	in love's darkest time	251
632	magnificent sight	251
633	when somewhere I hear	251
634	love all encaptured	251
635	my soul draws upward	252
636	can I ever tell	253
637	a grand intention	253
638	the heart of darkness	253
639	the art of darkness	253
640	her bold insistence	254
641	holding out to please	255
642	love's hard ruthlessness	255
643	love's enchoired voice	255
644	around a last sun	255
645	love's grand opening	256

646	presumptuous thought	257
647	so love promised me	257
648	should love adore you	257
649	so loving her now	257
650	the time of twilight	258
651	in the darkest times	259
652	fortune would have that	259
653	love open and kind	259
654	following my love	259
655	at finding some love	260
656	love's my sweet lady	261
657	some love is galant	261
658	afternoon delight	261
659	love stands a tower	261
660	my love is the night	262
661	love's some sweet lady	263
662	hails it with her tears	263
663	she guards her chaste thoughts	263
664	love can't hide from me	263
665	if she is burning	264
666	by breaking silence	265
667	tipsy turvy love	265
668	calm love's open hand	265
669	ever changing life	265
670	a sweet pirouette	266
671	she's holding my heart	267
672	that hot path of lust	267

673	startled unaware	267
674	love dabs at colors	267
675	with a warming heart	268
676	this sweet spot of earth	269
677	a glad rising mount	269
678	love's beautiful wings	269
679	stars shining above	269
680	so lingeringly	270
681	love flowing on air	271
682	clear skies all about	271
683	sure from here to there	271
684	love's lush full garden	271
685	a strong easing ease	272
686	my love's runaround	273
687	she floats to me	273
688	hatred and dark fear	273
689	then love will show me	273
690	roses by dozens	274
691	old loves found again	275
692	dwelling now on thens	275
693	dreams of loves long gone	275
694	dark demonstration	275
695	loves that will blossom	276
696	time spent in choice love	277
697	a love dear to me	277
698	those sweet words she moans	277
699	the lonely man knows	277

700	spring comes to them then	278
701	all love's memories	279
702	blinded by some blow	279
703	dancing in the rain	279
704	love calling me out	279
705	taking my love's hand	280
706	blooms sway in love's wake	281
707	is it love's belief	281
708	as if lighting strikes	281
709	wanting to own me	281
710	anytime rampant	282
711	on a dreaming night	283
712	love's gift in the past	283
713	drink rapt in love's time	283
714	still remembered times	283
715	love's ability	284
716	wonders have been told	285
717	so painterly then	285
718	love's lovely meaning	285
719	then eternity	285
720	love nests me surely	286
721	love casts its blessing	287
722	ample love reclines	287
723	love's full of fancies	287
724	never lasting long	287
725	she will be my all	288
726	love's illusion cast	289

727	*mildest growing love*	289
728	*beauty found by chance*	289
729	*to catch the tunings*	289
730	*please help me to find*	290
731	*love's light habitat*	291
732	*that bright glance from love*	291
733	*rewards of new love*	291
734	*love lumens lustrous*	291
735	*I hardly believe*	292
736	*time was when she'd watch*	293
737	*a golden evening*	293
738	*the ocean's depth*	293
739	*all love hopes, love's fears*	293
740	*a foreboding tone*	294
741	*love unrequited*	295
742	*love everlasting*	295
743	*like love's heights and depths*	295
744	*crazed wandering ways*	295
745	*in times of great joy*	296
746	*love burned all daylight*	297
747	*love calling to me*	297
748	*what has been we know*	297
749	*from the deepest depths*	297
750	*survey her domain*	298
751	*behold love's fair form*	299
752	*love will enthrall you*	299
753	*what our fired souls find*	299

754	love so elated	299
755	I do know it now	300
756	hard love could not wait	301
757	I desired it then	301
758	love didn't blind me	301
759	with harshening words	301
760	your love for me shines	302
761	so few have ever	303
762	if only I could	303
763	on nights so involved	303
764	loving you never	303
765	in love with you now	304
766	even more these days	305
767	love overreaches	305
768	please shoot me there where	305
769	he thinks about it	305
770	then you turn away	306
771	I might not say that	307
772	you make loving fun	307
773	may love always be	307
774	warm relationships	307
775	thrice upon a time	308
776	the finding of love	309
777	the increase of love	309
778	true love will not pass	309
779	love will always hold	309
780	give to us that love	310

781	if love's dreams give peace	311
782	to join us in love	311
783	love's noble nature	311
784	here's to lasting love	311
785	may love bless and keep	312
786	love beckons and holds	313
787	upholding spirits	313
788	faithful in support	313
789	garden of delights	313
790	visions of love's might	314
791	all love's tales to tell	315
792	never-ending peace	315
793	my love gives to me	315
794	the blessèd spring comes	315
795	love's sweet diadem	316
796	to lengths yet unknown	317
797	forever searching	317
798	in a golden time	317
799	some maybe believe	317
800	sleeping in love's night	318
801	passioned poets sing	319
802	lost love haunts as snow	319
803	holy constancy	319
804	to trumpet our love	319
805	the flowers of love	320
806	its mightiest stance	321
807	many quiet hours	321

808	*many and many*	*321*
809	*our grand love affair*	*321*
810	*love's warm jeweled arms*	*322*
811	*may love's vast bounty*	*323*
812	*my love welcomed me*	*323*
813	*charms so plenteous*	*323*
814	*love's largess offered*	*323*
815	*love's hard game to play*	*324*
816	*my love beckons me*	*325*
817	*love's tender April*	*325*
818	*spring is eternal*	*325*
819	*a sobering thought*	*325*
820	*longing ago sounds*	*326*
821	*close on bleak hard dreams*	*327*
822	*thoughts soaring with me*	*327*
823	*what dreams come to me*	*327*
824	*her pledge to me*	*327*
825	*all hail love's coming*	*328*
826	*love could promise me*	*329*
827	*breaking our joyful hearts*	*329*
828	*love's abrupt exit*	*329*
829	*love always conquers*	*329*
830	*always crimson cheeked*	*330*
831	*when it lastly came*	*331*
832	*a coming pitfall*	*331*
833	*felt love's wide array*	*331*
834	*our kneeling to love*	*331*

835	diadem for love	332
836	fairy fantasies	333
837	and thus the dawned light	333
838	coming with great speed	333
839	love will enfire us	333
840	to our emptiness	334
841	for me to hold love	335
842	easy to know it	335
843	with her joyful cries	335
844	my love sweeps me up	335
845	her sleep enchanting	336
846	for many moments	337
847	entune my high hopes	337
848	love's rush to my breast	337
849	a gentle rocking	337
850	a broad upturned smile	338
851	ethereal time	339
852	something of distance	339
853	love's so sombering game	339
854	love's hidden treasures	339
855	Barb asked me one time	340
856	I don't really know	341
857	I've now forgotten	341
858	in the end our loves	341
859	love have I not been	341
860	I did as I could	342
861	dear love it has been	343

862 Keats has inspired me 343
863 love in the end hid 343
864 find ardent romance 343
865 In service of love..344
866 A labor of love..345

1
green buds thrive in spring
love shapes our long years falling
moving back in time

2
I give you my love
hard true high and passionate
you held in my arms

3
in love's pure circumference
geometry burns colder
than hottest passion

4
for only true love
and all that can mean for two
leaving us breathless

5
never-changing love
still memories move in time
love holds its place still

6
summer's mellow months
love's made a dream of favor
warm hours in reprieve

7
when love's so perfect
when time passes slowly by
when our love is all

8
moving on in time
love's dance of days remembers
time's forgetfulness

9
days fly quickly past
fast changes move us forward
love will try to last

10
fall so short in love
a chilling time all too long
strain of love's colors

11
love knows its boundaries
those harsh words in haste speak ends
more words cannot save

12
your hand clasping mine
a warmth that spoke of our love
all emptiness now

13
winter walks at night
love's long ago memory
leaves no warm embrace

> 'Cause part of you pours out of me
> In these lines from time to time
> -- A Case of You
> Joni Mitchell

14
red on white canvass
splashes across dead spaces
love's void takes color

15
days fall into years
in love's still pure circumstance
for some perfect time

16
love asks no favors
only to be and let be
meaning everything

17
in fond remembrance
love gives over all its days
to warm colored times

18
what is more than love
since love can envelop all
ceasing at nothing

19
hate is more than love
burning bridges to ashes
in advance on love

20
hate is less than love
burning bridges to ashes
where love blooms again

21
never-changing love
still memories move in time
love holds its place still

22
when love's so perfect
when time passes slowly by
when our love is all

23
moving on in time
love's dance of days remembers
time's forgetfulness

24
days fly quickly past
fast changes move us forward
love will try to last

25
orange on gray canvass
love never can take lightly
night's coming darkness

26
never-changing love
still memories move in time
love holds its place still

27
not find true love here
will never wholly kiss you
careless of syntax

28
days fall into years
in love's still pure circumstance
for some perfect time

29
in warming to love
empty hearts give up their all
for love to make full

30
in silence love grows
brighter than the brightest star
love cannot do more

31
enduring all blows
love withstands harshest forces
a power so great

32
forget about love
love's mind changes easily
whenever it suits

33
a caress so soft
for all who seek to find it
in the end is love

34
if it's true love's blind
then why does it always tear
a path to my heart

35
love is blind to faults
overlooking everything
for what lies beneath

36
you see love is blind
or so the old saying goes
till it stabs your heart

37
love thrives to the end
taking root in waiting hearts
there to be consumed

38
if love were so true
then life would be beautiful
but just a moment

39
love is kind and true
making the most of your time
until it leaves you

40
when in love beware
false words and sweetest lies told
often deceive us

41
love chooses those whom
deserving of affection
run to embrace it

42
love cannot decide
fickleness without remorse
inconstant always

43
love may let us down
leaving unexpectedly
dropping us so fast

44
in the end with love
all may disappear like smoke
leaving emptiness

45
love will always look
for saddened hearts to lift up
a reason for hope

46
hollow sounds echo
all the feeling now is gone
was love nothing else

47
love is changeable
playing raucously and rough
then subdued and soft

48
though we may forget
at those times we feel secure
can love be our all

49
without love to heal
all wounds of past loves carried
would soon be fatal

50
when true love is lost
hatred's ugly head may rise
but love was still love

51
love's warm daylight hours
prove only that love sees not
its journey towards night

52
hate makes war on love
trying hard to beat it down
but love will still rise

53
then when love passes
an emptiness it leaves us
a void rarely filled

54
to love in the end
we give up an emptiness
that yearns to be filled

55
then hate spawns new fears
of love's clasp to be undone
in time for heartbreak

56
with nothing to lose
love will run wildly enough
for us to feel free

57
for some this is truth
love cannot take its slow time
in quick time it's found

58
love will stand steadfast
love fights to keep itself whole
love wins in the end

59
love moves on in time
carries time on its shoulders
time against an end

60
love weakens in those
who will never understand
why time won't stand still

61

if love can feel pain
even though threatened by time
love can still stand firm

62
breathe hope while you sleep
love still works magic on you
wake to new promise

63
dangerous and wild
love claws and tears at our hearts
rending our false hopes

64
love cannot be tamed
savage wild it rips and claws
leaving shredded dreams

65
love is perilous
traps set for romantic fools
ensnaring us all

66
if only our love knew
the tribulations whereby
we fight against time

67
when love's game is won
when true love is really ours
when time will stand still

68
blinding our reason
all sense and caution falter
when mad love steps in

69
give over all you have
drop everything you hold dear
love will show the way

70
if time healed all wounds
then love's hurt would disappear
wait for new heartbreak

71
distracting desire
love's a dream passing at night
lingering perfume

72
if it were easy
then all of us would value
love much less the more

73
lingering perfume
hints of love's reality
even in our dreams

74
even in our dreams
that perfect time of true love
lasting an instant

75
lasting an instant
fleeting love that might have been
never seen again

76
never seen again
a love so pure it blinds us
maybe once in life

77
maybe once in life
maybe that one love in life
may be missed by chance

78
may be missed by chance
that powerful love so chaste
it hardly can be

79
it can hardly be
love's knot a sacred promise
lasting forever

80
lasting forever
our love that always holds strong
strengthened through kind time

81
strengthened through kind time
by all things that hamper love
a journey for love

82
a journey for love
old age cannot ever lose
love that stands so strong

83
love that stands so strong
a barricade against loss
marking time with joy

84
marking time with joy
anniversaries of love
fresh celebrations

85
fresh celebrations
earned through holding onto love
each and every year

86
each and every year
great love will stay new and warm
mellowing the time

87
mellowing the time
love's experience runs deep
once can be enough

88
once can be enough
but many chances may come
distracting desire

89
who knew love's passing
would be all too quick and sure
leaving us not us

90
and at the end we
with all our love's sweet music
hear only echoes

91
no steel bars can stop
could ever contain our love
a cell sits empty

92
she embodies love
making every small caress
feel like the first one

93
first holding my hand
her touch of warming promise
hints enduring love

94
she dazzles dark ways
making love at black midnight
daylight's sure return

95
her love is my sun
brimming with a sparkling light
my heart shines with hers

96
she has all my love
holding it in sacred trust
for eternity

97
her love is like fire
burning me when we're apart
waiting for her kiss

98
should she leave me now
life would become stark wasteland
love completes my hours

99
when she turns the game
then she responds like cooled heat
then love's cards are played

100
she was once true love
then stroking my hot desire
finished all too soon

101
even at the end
she was kind as she could be
love's a hurting thing

102
she lives beyond love
standing light years from my heart
love gone forever

103
the brush of her hand
never again touching me
love is a dream now

104
If I tried harder
I'd have forgotten love's scent
if only I could

105
when love looks for us
when love finally finds us
then love settles in

106
if love cradles us
if our love holds on to us
then love keeps us safe

107
love's security
we wait hoping to be found
love's stability

108
love at any price
a sometime desperation
love cannot be bought

109
love is not for sale
that beat stirs our ready hearts
leaping beyond price

110
if only love would
last forever and beyond
impermanent love

111
love's sure permanence
leaves lovers wanting nothing
winning their soul's aim

112
love's impermanence
leaves lovers panting for more
to lose in the end

113
love can last enough
lovers not wanting for more
a warm ever glow

114
love cannot last long
if lovers are not constant
love lost through neglect

115
love makes no promise
love knows no point in promise
love knows only love

116
words make hot desire
tongues stir sensual voices
the language of love

117
all love's fitful dreams
fears of love's inconstancy
disappear at dawn

118
day's brilliant sunset
brings the secrets of darkness
that only love knows best

119
night's secrets warn love
to be constantly watchful
for bright dawn's new truths

120
of all of the kinds
the sweetest sort of all loves
is love not looked for

121
if love conquers all
then love is a true badass
that's not surprising

122
love's high barricades
fall before the willing hearts
of those who've no one

123
love and violence
a gun can't even stop love
Warren Zevon says

124
with love at first sight
the heart leaps in the moment
to find its new bond

125
two separate hearts
when they do find each other
join as one in love

126
what do you call love
Lou Reed has said in a song
it comes down to trust

127
where is love hidden
it is not easily found
why is it so hard

128
of those loves gone by
I've lived among the memories
and tried to forget

129
when love looks away
the heart knows it will soon break
and pain will walk in

130
romantics believe
love at first sight can be real
at least once in life

131
a September thought
love once new has now grown old
Paul Simon once wrote

132
all you need is love
Lennon's famous pronouncement
love is all you need

133
only preachers talk
Love and Rockets likes to say
about love today

134
Willie Nelson's song
only memories remain
love's dying ember

135
love's true bluish light
till it's a pain in the ass
Blondie's riding high

136
Joni Mitchell sings
about having looked at love
it's all illusion

137
love is for the strong
love hurts like a stove that burns
Gram Parsons once said

138
of all things likely
only love can break your heart
as Neil Young has it

139
Young also says love
will endure and break down hate
love and only love

140
it's only my love
who takes my heart and holds it
in her careful hands

141
in her careful hands
my love takes my lightened heart
her intent to please

142
her intent to please
I bless love stealing my heart
setting it apart

143
setting it apart
my true love then sometimes leaves
hides in a new breast

144
hides in a new breast
love leaving me so lonely
never to regain

145
never to regain
love that may be roaming free
still I seek it now

146
still I seek it now
true love that was lost to find
cannot always hide

147
cannot always hide
love bends from my waiting arms
away from me still

148
away from me still
from time to time love's sad way
fly so far afield

149
fly so far afield
love gone wild and free to roam
rarely coming home

150
rarely coming home
love ranging other new hearts
coming not to me

151
coming not to me
a love long gone forgets me
leaves no hope for me

152
leaves no hope for me
a love once won and then lost
remembers nothing

153
with a love gone by
there's a ghost in every room
or so I have heard

154
the heart knows true love
recognizes a true love
if it is true love

155
love meets resistance
love meets harsh opposition
love still conquers all

156
love's clear and pure tone
a music beyond music
echoes in the heart

157
the strong music of love
knows not of an earthly scale
climbing unknown heights

158
love knows no music
it cannot sing in good time
melodiously

159
meet love halfway since
in romantic confusion
love flies to your arms

160
love makes plain intent
to storm the staunch walls of hate
damn hostility

161
love gives no warning
a sore time to leave may come
nothing left to say

162
we all know it's true
love comes with no guarantee
a heart sometimes breaks

163
never holding back
love cannot stand idly by
winning near the goal

164
love hurts and love kills
love can overpower us
leaving us for dead

165
if love could happen
I wish we'd be lovers now
you held in my arms

166
we once were lovers
even though it didn't work
I still think of you

167
love's a healing thing
a balm for all searing burns
soothing every scar

168
love's a drastic thing
whiplashing your head around
making your brain mush

169
love's a noisy thing
slamming a door in your face
when you least expect

170
love's a lively thing
so indefatigable
so energetic

171
love's a colored thing
sometimes a brilliant rainbow
ablaze in rainfall

172
love's a drastic thing
throwing high drama at you
all the world's its stage

173
love's a brittle thing
crumbling to dust in your hand
as it slips away

174
love's a hearty thing
holding all ends together
an enduring bond

175
love's a hurtful thing
full of heartbreak and desire
leaving you breathless

176
love's a manic thing
takes you to the very top
slams you on the floor

177
love's an active thing
searching you out at all times
watching out for you

178
love's a passive thing
waiting for you to find it
hoping you succeed

179
love's a wondrous thing
falling from out of the blue
unexpectedly

180
love's a heady thing
takes you soaring far away
to a breathless height

181
love's a fruitful thing
bearing your soft soul aloft
bursting into bloom

182
love's a baffling thing
spiriting our hearts away
into blissful mystery

183
love's a wondrous thing
hanging on with all its might
in a soft caress

184
love's a hurting thing
burning searing hot to scar
a jilted lover

185
loves a gentle thing
rocking your heart back and forth
singing lullabies

186
with love 's doubt I have
no right to couple myself
with you in thought's deed

187
love's a caustic thing
rubbing us the worst wrong way
ever grating us

188
love if to be found
shall I see one to surpass
past lovers long gone

189
love's a reckless thing
that bull in the china shop
breaking everything

190
the slope so steepend
all the water between us
love's precarious

191
love's a careful thing
moving warily forward
guarding each action

192
in search of love I
reach in places near me
touching each for one

193
love's a brutal thing
twisting your heart like a rag
wringing in the pain

194
love's sole fault to miss
my chances that have always
been the ones behind

195
love's a tender thing
caressing all it touches
so soft with its stroke

196
love is blown to me
the wind's in a sulky fit
spiriting her past

197
love's an artful thing
stepping carefully around
waiting to trap you

198
love's blasted going
seeing how in times like this
my soul will cry out

199
love's a funny thing
high laughter makes the heart soar
smiles that make you ache

200
the women you've known
you tell them how you love them
wanting forever

201
love's a saddening thing
breaking hearts both left and right
leaving loneliness

202
in love's high fever
from want of regular rest
all night to wrestle

203
love's a curious thing
peeking under the covers
nosing around you

204
in love's fine passion
do you not hear the high sea
beat its breast for you

205
love's a serious thing
wanting only faithfulness
hating flightiness

206
rumors of demise
stoke eternal whisperings
love's safe kept instead

207
love's a wanting thing
wanting all it can possess
wanting always more

208
when love is so kind
in such gentle temper found
beware the backlash

209
love's a tender thing
mixing memory and desire
for a dear lost heart

210
I've had many loves
single the one that is true
I knew the first time

211
love's a distant thing
standing off outside of view
making no promise

212
of all that's in play
of all our alternatives
to love's soft calling

213
longing for your love
wondering a wounded past
love's a wistful thing

214
spring flowers bring renewal
and as if a budding grove
love's growth is assured

215
vigorous of heart
pounding out a forceful beat
love's a mighty thing

216
the promise of my love
of glorious great intent
all gone to nothing

217
love's a comely thing
attractive in appearance
pleasing in its path

218
every love that's passed
brings all your present troubles
to a blinding close

219
not meant for your ears
whispers down winding hallways
love's a secret thing

220
for love gone wanting
then banish all the wide world
to find what love's left

221
boldly strutting by
loud and showy of intent
love's a lurid thing

222
love astonishes
where that is our hearts deepen
stirring up the soul

223
love's a vivid thing
well defined and so vibrant
holding you in thrall

224
love's purest embrace
which all hunt after in life
catching so little

225
love's a dazzling thing
radiant in light's texture
blinding you with joy

226
longing for a heart
endeavor of the present
hope for love inspired

227
love's a rapturous thing
holding you in embraced bliss
enchanting through time

228
love lasting for good
the heirs of eternity
look to history

229
love's a stubborn thing
holding on to you always
never letting go

230
for you my dear love
an old flame burns in my heart
lighting love's dark way

231
if I did love you
then words could not express it
but these are for you

232
that the past were now
to hear love's sweet conversing
azure as ocean

233
at first sight of you
my love for you blossomed
flower beyond price

234
love reared my desire
truth is I have been in such
a sweet state of mind

235
to love you always
made me crazier by far
than life without you

236
often in love's chance
a finer wisdom presides
making a fair match

237
my life without you
came true in the worst of ways
leaving me empty

238
when love's on the run
a nettle leaf or two in
your soft and sweet bed

239
a life without love
when you are gone forever
is like no life lived

240
in love forever
spirit fevered contraries
speak never again

241
and when it's over
love is kind of like the blues
without the music

242
with love spinning round
reeling in a world of hope
drives my confused mind

243
love is a small gift
given with an open heart
to help us find grace

244
to help us find grace
love holds hands in a soft rain
painting a rainbow

245
painting a rainbow
choose from a brilliant palette
all of love's colors

246
all of love's colors
create a pane of stained glass
beyond mere beauty

247
beyond mere beauty
in love we find the essence
of all we hold dear

248
of all we hold dear
love is the most precious thing
love should never cease

249
love should never cease
holding on to what is prized
in its strong tight arms

250
wanting nothing more
we pursue love in circles
a fine way to play

251
love drives sleep away
this dark quiet that we seek
is unknown to love

252
with love comes marriage
giving us the bright promise
of lifelong passion

253
wedding vows commit
give us hope of lasting bliss
love's eternal bond

254
in this life we seek
some vision of permanence
an eternal love

255
eternal love is
all in all to all lovers
grasping for love's truth

256
love's truth is nothing
without the will to withstand
time's pulsing pressure

257
to solve love's mystery
clues scattered along the way
for us to unknot

258
young love does not know
silence speaks abiding truth
for seasoned lovers

259
love is born where you
shorn of life's dull illusions
quit false affections

260
one truth about love
it can appear from nowhere
giving no warning

261
in no way does love
know there is no other way
than not to show forth

262
for some just one chance
for some a million chances
I still wait for love

263
some lovers might say
that love is not blind enough
flaws slowly revealed

264
love tears at my heart
warning me about this one
one who got away

265
if love doesn't hurt
if love doesn't burn you down
then it isn't love

266
would that love would speak
telling me of those deceits
love set up for me

267
in the days gone by
when love was going strong
I thought of no end

268
I thought of no end
to a love that seemed so real
I almost touched it

269
I almost touched it
that one love in a lifetime
nearly in my grasp

270
nearly in my grasp
fading away before me
love's dear memories

271
love's dear memories
nothing I can remember
if only I could

272
if only I could
harder to find than pure gold
a love beyond price

273
a love beyond price
is free for all who seek it
if it can be found

274
what will be with love
will be a culmination
of sweet what have beens

275
if it can be found
I would hope to find it soon
love light my way home

276
love light my way home
someone stands ahead of me
shining in the night

277
shining in the night
my love's like a brightening dream
visions of the sun

278
visions of the sun
are like my love's appearance
warming in my arms

279
love is wonderful
for all of its frustrations
love can't be surpassed

280
love is terrible
with all of its frustrations
is it worth the pain

281
it is worth the pain
with all of its frustrations
love is wonderful

282
to love or love not
a lopsided conundrum
step into the fire

283
that fiery passion
love's first terrific blooming
dripping with frenzy

284
burning with passion
love takes its toll on us all
leaves a thirst for more

285
minding my love's way
with passionate attention
I take care of her

286
worried she may leave
I watch my love's reactions
gauging every move

287
my love is sweet rain
falling onto every bloom
each clear drop a jewel

288
love's a thunderstorm
pouring windblown slashing rain
each drop cutting me

289
love's a freezing snow
blowing in a winter storm
longing for the spring

290
my love's a warning
at your own point of peril
dream of the future

291
If my love offends
I simply overlook it
my own faults so great

292
love in the present
beats love lost in the past
the future's unknown

293
love is imperfect
perfection is impossible
even true loves fail

294
every love's different
to suffer in all alike
is sometimes one's fate

295
a full quiver slays
many beasts in the jungle
but then it's not love

296
to sustain my love
I need protection from fate
to make this one last

297
many fractured loves
sharded in covetousness
foretell of lean times

298
love in the moment
what's to be the end of this
only hard chance knows

299
after I gambled
I found love a remedy
who would think it so

300
to come to that point
in only a short month
true love did once bloom

301
I said I loved her
I don't know how it was so
I told something false

302
forgotten by love
we too much in solitude
forget to live life

303
proing and conning
love may fool us in some way
seeing just one side

304
in love's strangling thrall
sensitive and revealing
moments straggle forth

305
love seeks to placate
your favorite little wants
madly to fulfill

306
love we have been so
little together that you
seem to avoid me

307
when love is real we're
able to rejoice in things
that are beautiful

308
if love's on the wing
I hope I will be able
to rise close to it

309
love is so reserved
it should tell me about all
it hopes me to win

310
we surely become
intimately acquainted
with our hopes for love

311
and as we grow up
true love comes upon us in
many different forms

312
once or twice I have
confided in love as though
my sweet friend for life

313
when I saw you last
your love for me had faded
as an old friend gone

314
often heartbroken
I've lived a reclusive life
among love's cursed ruins

315
love has taken me
to many treasured places
in the realms of gold

316
love's sometimes written
hard letters that break my heart
telling me sad truths

317
love could tell me now
about how it conquers all
to remind me, please

318
love sees with bright eyes
looks with pleasure on times past
that may come again

319
forgotten at last
you will leave us far behind
love's failure in time

320
If love were once mine
I would be disappointed
at losing it now

321
a cursory glance
and you would never have thought
my love had grown wild

322
steeped in no love here
now me us turn to the sea
evermore to yearn

323
love finds me mindful
in this fine part of the year
a season of hope

324
in a giving time
winning some little fondness
from love's too hard world

325
to storm on my love
in truth the great elements
are mean comforters

326
with love unruly wild
the whole world sets upon
open hopeful hearts

327
love takes its chances
to make such a one as I
forget hard-shipped times

328
the ultimate love
is enjoyment not to be
put into mere words

329
placing our love held
in our pure imaginings
we please ourselves well

330
I'm in this fine game
where my love may pick and choose
another damned one

331
all love engenders
for those hoped to be in love
is an anxious mind

332
for us a caged love
which I'm sure you would not want
when love should roam free

333
A false love would fail
being blown up without wings
to hold it aloft

334
when love comes to us
when we have acquired that strength
then we'll not falter

335
with little chance of
anything in life to soothe
we pray for true love

336
if a heart finds me
her happiness is sacred
to me as her love

337
if a new love comes
then are sweet songs gladly sung
soaring in my heart

338
in finding new love
all can be completely changed
for good or for ill

339
when my true love comes
there's a possibility
I will live inside her

340
love's game lies ahead
for anyone to conquer
if you learn to play

341
if love were so clear
if only love played fairly
love could be so kind

342
perhaps you have found
love not to be easily
won in this short life

343
to feel love's true fire
better to seize blazing flames
than to touch embers

344
love stood still in time
as I passed and then turned back
she had left me here

345
hope for good fortune
that makes us heirs of all love's
heartfelt ambitions

346
in love's soft embrace
to breathe all the more freely
such rarified air

347
to run here and there
for love's sake could be madness
with a vexing end

348
to find love at last
a most great promise keeper
all else means nothing

349
a path to pleasure
dear love we will go with you
on that sunlit way

350
dear love's secrets are
not used to keep me silent
while seeking rapture

351
love I'll tell you what
if you can find me someone
soon I'll sing your name

352
then I had not seen
all that love could offer me
so missed that one chance

353
light and lively we
frolic in the fairy power
of love's charmed kindness

354
love taking all forlorn
with the magic hand of chance
scooping up sorrow

355
fair soul of an hour
love's magnificent being
watched for just awhile

356
with night skies coming
do love and heat to nothing
darkly sink away

357
love sports in the sun
living before its falling
in dark wasted time

358
when love's in full bloom
running blissfully to watch
over its beauties

359
no rude disturbance
can make true love hesitate
to deal hard with it

360
should love chance high seas
of rare enchantment hear then
the calm of sweet tides

361
a wedding vow sounds
of solemn bonds a thousand
years and more of love

362
a brief affair would
make fierce music and wild
uproar if love stayed

363
love's sweet voice is soft
a rose full bloomed and fragrant
bearing light petals

364
on a gentle breeze
love's whisper of peace and truth
leaves our hearts enthralled

365
love's sidelong glance tells
of more fine words to unfold
before our time's through

366
I've always heard that
love is this world's truest joy
but do I know this

367
only favored ones
breathe love's high and holy prayer
whisper their worship

368
when lover's hearts freeze
never to breathe pure serene
then lover's hearts fail

369
one warm gentle word
real compassion in love's name
showing us our path

370
it's love's path to know
only the way we show it
a real truth less known

371
love holds on not fast
the blood rushes from our hearts
to find jealousy

372
with love tearing deep
a blind singleness of aim
hearts are ripped apart

373
in love's tough game play
the push pull of strong desires
all to strain a heart

374
we would give the world
another heart for love's game
to play with even if

375
in love's toughest times
the poetry of the heart
is never truly quelled

376
though sometimes it ends
love always happily takes
us into its arms

377
love stretched out at ease
beautiful yet to behold
warming to embrace

378
love sends its soft dream
to exhausted hardened hearts
divine arousal

379
to grow its progress
love's in an envious race
never tiring still

380
in indifference
love with calm uneager face
looks away from me

381
fully blinded I
fell into a swooning love
that enveloped me

382
love shot its arrow
and struck a hottest desire
which did enslave me

383
I wandered awhile
looking for love in places
it could not be found

384
then love did find me
opening my heart fully
blood rushing so fast

385
all loves who've passed by
in chance encounters I've had
are always still dear

386
sick to lose love now
I try my best to keep you
nearest to my heart

387
and the truest heart
is formed of genuine love
the best kind of heart

388
love is to behold
a ceaseless dream to fancy
a golden splendor

389
love will surely come
a sweet lullaby passing
to arouse our dreams

390
love's a drop of light
a bright spark of boundless hope
a soon burning blaze

391
the joy of love glows
melting into radiance
luminous aura

392
solid permanence
drawn together over time
now immortal love

393
why then confusion
lost in legion thoughts of love
where reason does fade

394
love's coming rapture
a hope beyond the shadow
of again dreamed dreams

395
love's oh so gentle
a delightful thing to have
no matter how rough

396
love can make you do
whatever it wants you to
like a puppet strung

397
some heavy lightness
love's made of constant clashings
stubborn to resolve

398
love does amaze in
saddening you at odd times
or yielding great joy

399
dazzled eyes glowing
love in its early stages
a fire sparkling bright

400
love's gone and what's left
a sea nourished with your tears
despair abounding

401
words not meant for you
those longings not requited
a love unfulfilled

402
in love's increasing
sighs will turn to gentle moans
to arouse love's heirs

403
in the course toward joy
when mere hope becomes real dream
love's flame burns white hot

404
in current dawning
love breaking on the bright shore
a fair new bauble

405
that love is now mine
in every way it gleams
dull a loveless world

406
dreamless morning light
asks if that same night passed
in yearning for love

407
when the joys of love
plainly in each face do glow
then we gaze on bliss

408
in dear times now passed
my love I did much more praise
sad now to step aside

409
now long forgotten
that was our love's golden time
lost along the way

410
my sweet love rose up
seemed taking flight for heaven
then my hopes did end

411
in my dreams I dream
all that I may hope of them
love to enchant them

412
when my spirit's weak
then love has left me again
offering no hope

413
when love has been there
the joys of all my long life
have brought me to bliss

414
loves blazing by me
triumphs of old romances
and loses so dear

415
with each passing love
shadows haunting fairily
and moonbeams gleaming

416
radiant visions
love's mad rush to heartfelt joy
leaving us panting

417
for all you desire
a time will be right for love
coming to climax

418
she was kind to me
fed me many a false hope
plumped love with sweet lies

419
she says she loves me
In sometimes words I believe
she does deceive me

420
for the hoped truth is
marriage is not an ending
but love's beginning

421
if the truth be told
the one constant in love is
love's inconstancy

422
if amid tumult
love continues to flourish
then we've found true love

423
do we choose our love
or does real love seek us out
finding us at last

424
love looks not with eyes
but with the mind she says though
I would disagree

425
love's chaos in haste
is said to be just a child
blind and winged both

426
the truth of it this
that sex and love together
aren't a simple bond

427
love's sublime being
ecstasy beyond reason
what alone love knows

428
with love's speaking now
listen to this adoring
a call from within

429
with my heart pounding
oh my love to you alone
I walk in my dreams

430
and blissful is he
whom such happiness does find
in love forever

431
ascend highest heights
a frenzy of heated dreams
love's feverish heart

432
pale love sickly stood
panting for a chance gone by
and her eyes were wild

433
just beyond my reach
love why do you linger so
teasing me again

434
she did not speak but
looked at me as if she loved
oh how looks deceive

435
that night's perfect love
saying she was mine for good
fades farther away

436
unreflecting love
not caring how you treat us
playing your hard game

437
of love it is said
never did its course run smooth
but such sweet rewards

438
in fast times of joy
hopes do thrive in the moment
love matures quickly

439
pen and paper then
I wish I had those letters
her words of love gone

440
love I'm here waiting
I got some sweet Rolex dreams
but I'm lost in time

441
love's warming embrace
fills with superior bliss
a heart now taken

442
when love breaks down doors
what pleasures rise stronger
to storm lonely hearts

443
a holy message sent
on fleet love's flowing wings
hails all worshippers

444
love can open eyes
if our lives are but a dream
to love's arousal

445
when new love takes wing
soaring to its highest heights
blissful scenes unfold

446
when love's flame burns bright
then imagined pleasures glow
small in light of this

447
let love in dark skies
among the blistering stars
burn brighter by far

448
love soon puts to flight
all manner of despairing
dark dreams and dread night

449
with love's great power
dark clouds so fast arising
dispel in no time

450
whirling us away
new love's rapid coming on
a grand confusion

451
how I recovered
I cannot now remember
but love had lost me

452
memories of love
slip through my fingers like so
many grains of sand

453
love in now old times
all fairy magic sometimes
reconstructed myths

454
of long timeless love
short come the days remaining
time works this quick way

455
lost along the way
praying for love's great power
wholly sinners all

456
bright stars flash so cold
bright jewels lighting dreams of love
bright lights far too high

457
so nearing true love
many steps to pass along
still biting my tongue

458
survey love's pathway
so too much of cold bleak air
breathing fitful steam

459
the red leaves rustling
fall's gold air hints of home and
love at near distance

460
a stammered word heard
love's some uttered friendliness
holding trembling hands

461
try finding some love
hiding in those twisting turns
running fast ahead

462
stuttering desire
love's words light fires of high hope
eloquent distress

463
strong passion's embrace
love held once in gentler arms
now so tightly wrapped

464
blinded by desire
stumbling toward their desperate goal
the fated find love

465
strangled in mid-air
those who've been long in love's hold
do not wait for breath

466
take me to love's bounds
let me learn the real endgame
find me the finish

467
start the mad shouting
let the wild music wander
where our love awaits

468
love's a blessed song
a line of glorious tune
a rapt harmony

469
wandering down paths
so many startling wonders
show me love's slow curves

470
my spirit rising
highest heights have I to fly
seeking love's zenith

471
groping past the gloom
love cannot live in darkness
reaching for the light

472
some distant discord
bodes ill to seek an old love
in the present time

473
love whispered to me
of sweet passion to be mine
just for the asking

474
love once said to me
that my chance would come again
it has been so long

475
love in the small hours
a candle lights past midnight
time's passing passion

476
in long solitude
unkind love did let me dwell
counting my dark hours

477
if it should pass me
let it not be so that love
runs too fast to catch

478
now my love has passed
murky in my memory
dying now away

479
a steepening climb
finding love's high cherished seat
breathing rarest air

480
nature's hardest test
to find and to secure love
all of my spent life

481
love lifts me upward
boosting me to crest the clouds
of purest serene

482
love swiftly follows
when chance changes direction
for another heart

483
if it were the case
that love should run to me now
it would surprise me

484
the Ishiharas
love beyond a galaxy
so far far away

485
innocent love comes
shyly stepping toward me now
hushed as it is pure

486
love's pictures play out
images of thoughts defined
in deep mystery

487
tentative in deed
before a huge leap of faith
love must be quite sure

488
imagined great love
is my soul's brightest pleasure
in times of dark hope

489
in love's purest form
highest bliss of our being
a longed for desire

490
in love a bright match
two kindred spirits in flight
from an unreal world

491
with greatest promise
this way your love came to me
a fine nothingness

492
I've heard it said that
two hearts are better than one
love gave me just one

493
loving you always
I look back on joyful times
now solitary

494
love's fading embers
of dazzling times grown colder
a darkening fire

495
I've come to that point
this last stage presents no hope
of love awaiting

496
now so sweet love has
lingered long on soft moonlit
shores of lapping waves

497
that time when fairy
dust will glow with love's wonder
at the fall of night

498
could only lost love
close out the moon's brightened rays
so starred peace would come

499
nothing of love would
drive my cheerful heart away
during vibrant times

500
love's longing victims
biting tongues until they bleed
hoping to fall prey

501
hoping for some love
stepping lightly round and round
playing the fool's game

502
love's first soft footsteps
make their path through verdant ways
seeking plush meadows

503
hailing your advance
love's making way for you now
a crowning glory

504
rare purified gold
distilled aphrodisiac
love's shining essence

505
a grand profusion
vast fields of radiant flowers
are love's lavish haunt

506
fading fast away
through the waves a ruby glow
love's path past the edge

507
love's sensuousness
that voluptuous figure
those alluring looks

508
love's seductive stare
hints of sensual pleasures
dreamed carnal desires

509
find a love that stays
a proposition for you
gamble with your heart

510
truly wondrous love
fairest of all the flowers
blooming crazily

511
in my memory
so fair some loves never were
gone now to strangers

512
love so draws my eye
its hot smoking flames desire
forget clear thinking

513
to find perfect love
waiting just for me to come
luxurious dream

514
gently love did come
softly calling out my name
whispering of fire

515
hinting pains to come
prickling thorns of rose stem
love's gracious warning

516
a strange compression
growing in intimacy
love's tightening grip

517
if a love does fade
to remember everything
burdens to be borne

518
fiery yesterdays
kindle only ashes now
now love has grown cold

519
with that chance meeting
a budding new love does grow
blossoms in my heart

520
her long dark black hair
hanging so to shade her eyes
mysterious love

521
the glories of love
come upon us too little
we long for those times

522
long are we seekers
lost on our pathway to love
so do we wander

523
love's burning passion
an incense for the senses
a smokey sweet scent

524
in love we do bound
to meet the dawn of bright day
certain all is right

525
love may call to us
soft voiced and young and playful
inviting us home

526
in love we may seek
to adorn ourselves in light
clothed in sunning warmth

527
high hopes of sweet love
to taste those lofty pleasures
bursting ripe desires

528
a calling to believe
that I shall ever be blessed
praying now for love

529 a plan that's fulfilled
laid in sure simplicity
love's clear destiny

530
there may be times when
love cannot grow much stronger
having come so far

531
tried and so tired
the ways to bliss exhausted
love was scarcely found

532
dreaming I might love
someone beautiful as you
I stood thunderstruck

533
seeking love this way
with my few poor offerings
seems a vain attempt

534
love's glance cools me now
enough to make me stand still
chilled by memories

535
all my grand conquests
all my old triumphs in love
all are behind me

536
love beckoned me once
I refused so foolishly
a fortune misread

537
singing love's strong bond
canting that curve of music
heard by so few now

538
just barely touching
love's whispering silk domain
a heavenly grace

539
starry nights so clear
love rounding on a soft beam
of incandescence

540
burning hazily
those memories now of us
love's fiery moments

541
we were pure and shone
with love so then unspoken
that it would not fade

542
I dreamt that love came
adorable illusion
plaything of the mind

543
sometimes losing love
stalks me like a hunted one
and I cannot hide

544
icing love crackled
your winter steps walked away
leaving me so cold

545
crafted light and shade
love grows in the assemblage
of artful design

546
love's worn and tired prints
reproductions cheaply framed
in gilt now reposed

547
lost love's fading glow
a moondrop splashed on blue grass
going now to gray

548
in love's swift high stream
two shadows flow together
destined for the sea

549
searing our senses
burning trace of passion lost
a love's embrace gone

550
so hard to believe
love's gone around me again
truly unarranged

551
a romantic quest
true love's quietest moments
kept safe for hard times

552
in memory traced
oh the sweet times of my loves
remembered fondly

553
a joyous delight
fair love's shimmering angel
now flown to my side

554
love's intentioned heart
leading us to tight embrace
assures we hold fast

555
promised fruition
the blossoming of our love
comes not easily

556
that winged messenger
love softly glides to my heart
finding me waiting

557
now a newfound love
overcoming past despair
bringing me to life

558
when love comes near me
reaches out so tenderly
then I touch heaven

559
love long flown away
some silent cry in the night
breaking from my heart

560
I lost my love then
my heart was not spared at all
keen separation

561
when love will show me
soft visions rare and mild
peace comes upon me

562
unpracticed lovers
never fully comprehend
how old their desires

563
flown love stops my heart
winged away without goodbyes
leaving me breathless

564 those chaste devotions
to find love's holiest times
are smoldering prayers

565
those slow burning prayers
before love's fires soar full blown
are soft kindling sighs

566
all should step forward
fascinated by love's chance
curious what may come

567
my love lost in time
a fall from some kind of grace
never recovered

568
mesmerized by you
then bound up in love's rapture
soon a broken spell

569
love stirs skipped heartbeats
memories that stop my breath
and send me reeling

570
You will not know why
love stands stone silent, still, high
and so very cold

571
stunned backward by love
so slightingly too harshly
with no soothing hand

572
love's shy sidelong glance
opens up a bright discourse
pleasing curves of light

573
smooth rhythms in time
love's finely tapered fingers
playing on my skin

574
running away fast
fickle love now taking flight
has not lost me yet

575
unfolding petals
love lush and luxuriant
beware pricking thorns

576
sweetest love appears
seemingly sent to save me
from endless shadow

577
love's variety
some do surely thrive upon
but by no means all

578
the faintest motion
slow love fans a meagre flame
builds a savage fire

579
love serves all delights
conquer the variety
fair kaleidoscope

580
fantasy of light
playing out love's brilliant game
breathing crystal air

581
round of love's potion
a drink to our affection
draft me to the brim

582
a toss of the dice
and a curious bending
of love's gaming rules

583
never-ending love
with all its great obstacles
pushing you away

584
love lifted me up
I felt feather light and free
a gentle landing

585
led by sacred vows
stepping into paradise
I search for my love

586
searching for some love
many joys in visions came
vast apparitions

587
lost relationships
surely none would have it so
to be without love

588
when love is so strong
radiant intensity
powerful passion

589
passionate spirit
made to defy barriers
love stands resolute

590
now love's latter days
to be spent in greater love
than love's beginning

591
what makes love turn so
into such an attitude
that leaves us wanting

592
breaking hearts like glass
snapping roses' thorned stems
are these love's delights

593
imagined heaven
love's angel choir will burst forth
to sing such wonder

594
on love's gentle might
poets interminably
spend fierce words of praise

595
some poets will boast
to any old audience
their great tales of love

596
lost love's chilled hands grope
we cannot feel for the cold
all sentiment lost

597
move out and away
my sad heart gone wandering
hailed with new love's cries

598
an abandoned love
from its joyless self no thrill
derives once it's gone

599
had I lived in awe
of love's immortal spirit
then would I have loved

600
love's hot amber flame
burned its brightest in those times
when it burned anew

601
in our sometime past
love did sparkle and dazzle
feeding hungry hearts

602
for all that's heart longed
for all that seems almost near
for all blazing love

603
floating forever
in love's light air suspended
all one melody

604
as I lay dreaming
luxuriously sleeping
love came on tiptoe

605
now more than ever
love bless me with your presence
or I will be lost

606
in my distress now
love cares not to ease my mind
as she forgets me

607
of neglected love
I sometimes have been guilty
though I've met the same

608
oh dissembling love
for all you've done to confuse
be blind and wingless

609
how was I to know
that time she looked back at me
love was on the run

610
You think you've found it
that once in a lifetime find
then love looks away

611
only love could know
I would just twice be moved
flying to their arms

612
in moments of loss
I memorize searing pain
once love walks away

613
I looked on certain
for once love would hold me so
nothing could go wrong

614
at the bitter end
purposely abandoned I
say goodbye to love

615
for now or never
grasp love firmly by the hand
never letting go

616
so like common dust
so love did toss me aside
so did she leave me

617
a real love long lost
when I think about it now
darkens all my mind

618
You won't know her love
is the greatest you will have
until you lose her

619
I was wrong about love
any kind of fool could see
or so someone said

620
love's fondest embrace
with not one expectation
wraps warm around me

621
love don't let me go
turn me loose to feel again
that bone chilling freeze

622
in a playful mood
love taps me on the shoulder
tagging me along

623
a turn of shoulder
carved deep in strong shadowed light
shows love's graceful curves

624
to give two pleasure
ticking an infinite time
is love's chief delight

625
he awaits the spell
wondering when it will strike
some sweet lady's love

626
listening for a hint
of her coming to him now
a love all his own

627
a burning hot sleep
love comes to ease the fever
a more calming fire

628
fan me with wide wings
now revive a dying hope
love please bless me still

629
this is too far off
this love I seek forever
this bliss rarely near

630
love's crystal clear eyes
watching hope's horizoned dawn
help lost dreamers see

631
in love's darkest time
the mind reels at the joys that
fade too soon to black

632
magnificent sight
grandeur of the towers of love
inspired resplendence

633
when somewhere I hear
love's wild raucous revelries
I do remember

634
love all encaptured
a vision of spectrummed fire
brilliant pure array

635
my soul draws upward
taken to heights I've not known
love's tremendous grasp

636
can I ever tell
the enormity of love
in just so few words

637
a grand intention
to seek out love's lofty heights
a foolish design

638
the heart of darkness
love leaving me all alone
wandering nowhere

639
the art of darkness
love drawing its thick curtain
cloaking its best show

640
her bold insistence
love breaks down all barriers
making her way here

641
holding out to please
love's insisting that I come
along with her now

642
love's hard ruthlessness
handling heart's to be broken
like a mason stones

643
love's enchoired voice
musical inspiration
joyful to be heard

644
around a last sun
a single revolution
love falls to darkness

645
love's grand opening
draws greatest inspiration
from a partner's joy

646
presumptuous thought
that some love would come to me
if I wanted it

647
so love promised me
to affect me in some way
and left me wanting

648
should love adore you
she requires all kinds of thought
great care is needed

649
so loving her now
daring to burn at white heat
step into the fire

650
the time of twilight
her love forever haunting
my memories still

651
in the darkest times
those memories of her still
bring my love to tears

652
fortune would have that
memories still stir desire
love passing me by

653
love open and kind
beckoning us to join her
pulls us to her heart

654
following my love
a clear sunrise comes to mind
now a breaking dawn

655
at finding some love
my heart with pleasure dances
music tuned to pitch

656
love's my sweet lady
waiting now for me to come
waiting now for me

657
some love is galant
a tale of great chivalry
standing firm and proud

658
afternoon delight
love lies in a playful mood
sunning herself there

659
love stands a tower
wonder at its gentle might
ward of untold strength

660
my love is the night
tender on a moonlit isle
waves lapping gently

661
love's some sweet lady
pouring her perfume a balm
scenting all my dreams

662
hails it with her tears
does love going unfulfilled
grieving through the night

663
she guards her chaste thoughts
from love's lusty abandon
from inner desire

664
love can't hide from me
her happiest certainty
thunderous trembling

665
if she is burning
that fire flashing from her eyes
then love is ready

666
by breaking silence
love can show her cruelty
smashing quiet times

667
tipsy turvy love
imbibing my offerings
drunk off to the lees

668
calm love's open hand
reaching out for my tight grasp
desperate groping

669
ever changing life
love is never really gone
we will meet again
      (for Steve and LeeAnn and Sean Jones)

670
a sweet pirouette
my heart with pleasure turning
love's a measured dance

671
she's holding my heart
I'm trusting her gentleness
my love's tender care

672
that hot path of lust
may find a brilliant ending
where love burns brightest

673
startled unaware
by she who steals upon me
love's stealthy footsteps

674
love dabs at colors
paints a gradual portrait
so lingeringly

675
with a warming heart
love casts blushing radiance
rising inside me

676
this sweet spot of earth
this garden blooming so wild
love's grand profusion

677
a glad rising mount
now shows less and less the sun
happy in love's shade

678
love's beautiful wings
spreading so to enfold me
cloaking me in light

679
stars shining above
beauty of a silent night
love's quiet lightning

680
so lingeringly
love's caress before she goes
not wanting to leave

681
love flowing on air
darting diamonds of sunlight
from a cool blue sky

682
clear skies all about
untold visibility
will love search for me

683
sure from here to there
love making rounds round the moon
turns in its waiting

684
love's lush full garden
easy slopes and shading trees
waiting there for me

685
a strong easing ease
to view new love at full rest
while she waits for me

686
my love's runaround
widening to nothing gone
circles round circles

687
she floats to me
her fluttering wings entice
love glides to my bed

688
hatred and dark fear
and violence all around
can love save us yet

689
then love will show me
so that I can finally feel
with a heart like hers

690
roses by dozens
for a love gone by and lost
buy no breathing man

691
old loves found again
we had known them long ago
memories made flesh

692
dwelling now on thens
those loves of long pleasure
fortunes lost again

693
dreams of loves long gone
faded images of mind
casting soft shadows

694
dark demonstration
dimness of a twilight show
love overshadowed

695
loves that will blossom
these pleasant things of heaven
the wheel turns sometimes

696
time spent in choice love
gives many golden raptures
many joys to me

697
a love dear to me
I hope I will find someday
in some better times

698
those sweet words she moans
whispers of soft affections
too soon love steals back

699
the lonely man knows
that none tried harder wishes
love would seek him out

700
spring comes to them then
like a budding hopefulness
of new love to find

701
all love's memories
fairly some wander out of
fairylands forlorn

702
blinded by some blow
a love that is in need of
repair as my soul

703
dancing in the rain
under fresh summer showers
my love dips and sways

704
love calling me out
like something from far beyond
testing my resolve

705
taking my love's hand
thrilling with ardent pulses
beating just for me

706
blooms sway in love's wake
now forward gently bending
bowing their favor

707
is it love's belief
that joy is never-ending
never leaving us

708
as if lighting strikes
a white hot bolt from the sky
makes electric love

709
wanting to own me
the ambitious heat of love
burning down my heart

710
anytime rampant
when love mysterious wild
runs tearing my heart

711
on a dreaming night
love will sweep me up upon
the moon beaming air

712
love's gift in the past
a keepsake designed for me
lost along the way

713
drink rapt in love's time
on perfect nights a great draft
of deep sparkling wine

714
still remembered times
when love was so far away
but hearts were hopeful

715
love's ability
powers to bless and to sooth
great ills to assuage

716
wonders have been told
of love's curative power
legend far and wide

717
so painterly then
love's frame surely does portray
colors of desire

718
love's lovely meaning
the very definition
of learned distraction

719
then eternity
love that lasts to forever
take me from my here

720
love nests me surely
her sweetest comforts to share
a divine repose

721
love casts its blessing
like sky silver glitterings
over all who seek

722
ample love reclines
so fairy a place is known
a sight rarely seen

723
love's full of fancies
those soft feelings in my heart
placed with no regrets

724
never lasting long
desperately I will chase
ever fleeting love

725
she will be my all
love casts its spell on dreamers
those full of fancies

726
love's illusion cast
seen through lightening shadows
its soft glow creates

727
mildest growing love
so meek and kind and tender
take me to your breast

728
beauty found by chance
so desperately adored
yearning for her love

729
to catch the tunings
all love's strings are wound to sing
a voice most divine

730
please help me to find
the love that is high and great
and good and healing

731
love's light habitat
sunshine in a shady place
beaming with passion

732
that bright glance from love
her nod shines for me alone
an invitation

733
rewards of new love
that in the far distance seem
so close yet so far

734
love lumens lustrous
shining as a falling star
burning to the last

735
I hardly believe
lucky to be loved by you
I cross my fingers

736
time was when she'd watch
for me to come again and
kiss away love's fears

737
a golden evening
soft stars charm our hours spent
wrapped in warm love's arms

738
the ocean's depth
to the vastness of my love
compared is nothing

739
all love hopes, love's fears
turned to nothingness in time
for love's sure to grow

740
a foreboding tone
in love's mysterious voice
sings hard times ahead

741
love unrequited
today has us think about
what may never be

742
love everlasting
these words for you I write and
watch you turn away

743
like love's heights and depths
captured by the sky and sea
I stand in between

744
crazed wandering ways
bewildered by love's beauty
we beat on blindly

745
in times of great joy
love sings for all I've done to
kiss away her tears

746
love burned all daylight
watched the feathered gold of night
come light upon us

747
love calling to me
only to confuse me more
mysterious voice

748
what has been we know
only love knows what will be
a safe kept secret

749
from the deepest depths
soaring to the highest heights
the vastness of love

750
survey her domain
wonders of the sky and sea
love's geography

751
behold love's fair form
truly pleasing to the eye
soon to strike you blind

752
love will enthrall you
with spells and incantations
cast on you at will

753
what our fired souls find
in love's immortal spirit
is eternal life

754
love so elated
by her coming victory
vanquishing a heart

755
I do know it now
the grandeur that was my love
then beyond compare

756
hard love could not wait
for another time to say
goodbye to me then

757
I desired it then
I would love's fame venerate
so majestic she

758
love didn't blind me
so wholly I could not see
that you would leave me

759
with harshening words
my enchanted love loses
its fine mystery

760
your love for me shines
through misty clouds of few doubts
a sun just beyond

761
so few have ever
seen your love in all secret
spread before me here

762
if only I could
your love has here sat me down
to write my heartbreak

763
on nights so involved
your love intrudes on my sleep
waking me breathless

764
loving you never
meant more then than it does now
now that you leave me

765
in love with you now
confusion enters my mind
unexpectedly

766
even more these days
to love you now I've lost you
ever makes me ill

767
love overreaches
grasps for that distant finish
oftentimes a dream

768
please shoot me there where
love bonds me to some someone
else hot Cupid strikes

769
he thinks about it
the love of his life long gone
stares caught in the stars

770
then you turn away
in spite of my love for you
gone to another

771
I might not say that
her running me around makes
me a slave to love

772
you make loving fun
on the way to crescendo
it's all a great sport

773
may love always be
a remembered joy to me
a thing of beauty

774
warm relationships
may their lovingness increase
deepest affection

775
thrice upon a time
love came out to play with me
games I never won

776
the finding of love
can be a joy forever
with some good fortune

777
the increase of love
will be with careful tending
a stunning garden

778
true love will not pass
into bleakened nothingness
if we give our all

779
love will always hold
no matter the battering
if we will hold on

780
give to us that love
a sleep full of sweetest dreams
dreams awake made flesh

781
if love's dreams give peace
and health and quiet breathing
we rise to daylight

782
to join us in love
we're given these soft sashes
that blithely bind us

783
love's noble nature
will not let us be humbled
beggar our searching

784
here's to lasting love
tomorrow and tomorrow
aflame forever

785
may love bless and keep
a spirit all embracing
in spite of all bars

786
love beckons and holds
despite all adversity
a future so bright

787
upholding spirits
never swaying from purpose
ever constant love

788
faithful in support
offering our proffered hands
devoted to love

789
garden of delights
vistas goldened to behold
serene world of love

790
visions of love's might
barriers falling aside
witness to power

791
all love's tales to tell
poems for her to be written
await those untold

792
never-ending peace
tranquility beyond time
show to me this love

793
my love gives to me
the sun and the moon and all
these to prove our time

794
the blesséd spring comes
sprouting love's fresh flowers
for all to embrace

795
love's sweet diadem
a flowering band bonds us
blossoming passion

796
to lengths yet unknown
love grants nearly everything
her noble nature

797
forever searching
to find that love still unfound
paths ever winding

798
in a golden time
love belonged to a rich world
once upon some dream

799
some maybe believe
they've read or heard all love's tales
life always adds one

800
sleeping in love's night
wafting essence of perfume
wakened from some dream

801
passioned poets sing
love's lightning hot for all time
burning infinite

802
lost love haunts as snow
flurried against freezing glass
memories stood still

803
holy constancy
that love be always with us
small prayers to heaven

804
to trumpet our love
the very music of the name
sounds a harmony

805
the flowers of love
grow ever fresh before me
burst buds cherished all

806
its mightiest stance
love facing forth to advance
holds strong and steadfast

807
many quiet hours
has my dear love occupied
fantasy fulfilled

808
many and many
times too infinite to count
love has stood by me

809
our grand love affair
two hands held so hard it hurt
now left back somewhere

810
love's warm jeweled arms
universal touch of gold
wrapped in wealth untold

811
may love's vast bounty
be all about me when I
make my final peace

812
my love welcomed me
her generous arms outspread
now surrounding me

813
charms so plenteous
draw me into love's laced snare
wishing to be caught

814
love's largess offered
we harvest precious fruits through
our careful labor

815
love's hard game to play
hide and seeking secret hearts
sequestered from us

816
my love beckons me
to join with his longing heart
holding hands again

817
love's tender April
celebrates eternal spring
with fragrant gardens

818
spring is eternal
calling off the months to come
love's youthful gesture

819
a sobering thought
that spring love may airily
fly away too soon

820
longing ago sounds
gone to follow love as she
sings her faraway

821
close on bleak hard dreams
comes love's show of new dark dawns
disheartening me

822
thoughts soaring with me
wrapped in love's grand illusion
I die blissfully

823
what dreams come to me
so fairily wrought by her
love's beneficence

824
her pledge to me
by love's great renown
ended hollowly

825
all hail love's coming
longing to grasp offered hands
echoes down hallways

826
love could promise me
a seeming throng of women
my bolstered spirits

827
breaking our joyful hearts
shattering relationships
this love's dreaded course

828
love's abrupt exit
something never understood
as one consequence

829
love always conquers
hearts in quick anyways and
oftentimes will strut

830
always crimson cheeked
love paled for fear of my loss
a short ways coming

831
when it lastly came
love's quick end was all without
a single warning

832
a coming pitfall
with no opportunity
love's dear hand withheld

833
felt love's wide array
full in the middle of this
pleasantness profound

834
our kneeling to love
there stands a holy altar
for worship of her

835
diadem for love
hailing her glory with crown
of new flower bursts

836
fairy fantasies
of love's eternal coming
charm me to her arms

837
and thus the dawned light
reveals to us her secret
love's hidden bower

838
coming with great speed
brisk spirits might win love's eye
take them to her breast

839
love will enfire us
melt out our essence so fine
tear at our being

840
to our emptiness
love does not pour cheering toasts
telling of our loss

841
for me to hold love
to try too hard at grasping
Still I reach for her

842
easy to know it
that love was lost in her eyes
turned cold to my heart

843
with her joyful cries
love sings me a perfect song
her passion chaired

844
my love sweeps me up
to a place where all birds sing
hear their joyous song

845
her sleep enchanting
the silent workings of dawn
to wake with my love

846
for many moments
I stop to listen deeply
hear love's lullaby

847
entune my high hopes
the inspired breath of music
love sings in my heart

848
love's rush to my breast
feathering an open heart
bursting full headlong

849
a gentle rocking
her softly rich swellings are
love's tender lappings

850
a broad upturned smile
love's glee at passing me by
leaving me without

851
ethereal time
a gently kissed christening
love enters softly

852
something of distance
comes a deep and mellowed sound
love calls us to meet

853
love's so sombering game
venerable and subdued
cold disposition

854
love's hidden treasures
searching eyes all strain to see
winning near the goal

855
Barb asked me one time
if I'd ever repeated
any love haiku

856
I don't really know
if I've ever repeated
any love haiku

857
I've now forgotten
did I breathe love's pure serene
share in it ever

858
in the end our loves
with all their many facets
show us countless whims

859
love have I not been
of great service to you for
oh so long a time

860
I did as I could
of the days of love gone by
tell my whole story

861
dear love it has been
so many lines penned that I
might learn to hate you

862
Keats has inspired me
all love haiku praise to him
all failures to me

863
love in the end hid
veiling its grand adventure
leaving me to seek

864
find ardent romance
may true love always be yours
my fond wish for you

865
In service of love
I've dedicated my time
hoping it worthwhile

866
A labor of love
I dare to hope you've read my
humble love haiku

01.01.17: Well, today is the first day of my retirement, so it's the last day for my love haiku   866 is 501 more than I intended to write when I first started this project. I truly hope that you've enjoyed my efforts   May love and peace always be with you. Mahalo for reading.

Made in the USA
Monee, IL
18 October 2025